IMAGES
of America

MACON

In 1943, photographer Esther Bubley made a six-week bus trip across the United States to document the nation's transition from the poverty of the Great Depression to the frenzied activity of World War II for the Office of War Information. Here, she photographed an unidentified woman preparing to board a bus for Macon, where many men and women sought war jobs. (Library of Congress.)

ON THE COVER: The Procter & Gamble Manufacturing Company was one of Macon's largest employers in the early 20th century, and this 1926 image shows workers who've just received their Christmas baskets. This sort of industrial paternalism was fairly common at the time. (Middle Georgia Archives, Washington Memorial Library.)

IMAGES
of America

MACON

Stephen Wallace Taylor and Matthew Jennings

ARCADIA
PUBLISHING

Published by Arcadia Publishing
Charleston, South Carolina

Library of Congress Control Number: 2013940627

For all general information, please contact Arcadia Publishing:
Telephone 843-853-2070
Fax 843-853-0044
E-mail sales@arcadiapublishing.com
For customer service and orders:
Toll-Free 1-888-313-2665

Visit us on the Internet at www.arcadiapublishing.com

*To Macon and its people: May we be informed—but not enslaved—
by our past as we look toward the future with clear eyes*

CONTENTS

ACKNOWLEDGMENTS

No work of historical scholarship is entirely the creation of its authors, but a pictorial history is an extreme example of collective effort. Very few of the pictures that follow come from our personal collections. The archivists at Washington Memorial Library have been exceedingly generous during every step of the process; as the credits show, this book would not exist without the phenomenal holdings at that archive. Thanks especially to Muriel McDowell-Jackson, Willard Rocker, and James O'Neal, who handled requests verging on the absurd with professionalism and aplomb. Ocmulgee National Monument was quite generous as well; thanks to Lonnie Davis and Angela Bates for their assistance in those archives. The staff at the Cannonball House was accommodating, too. Many of the images came from the Library of Congress, a national treasure of the highest order. Sheron Smith of Middle Georgia State College provided access to some fine images of the campus. A special thank you to Michelle Klingaman, whose moral support was invaluable and whose careful management of resources made it possible for the Department of History and Political Science at Middle Georgia State College to generously subsidize the cost of scanning these images.

Lastly, Margaret Anne Shannon provided a deft hand and a keen eye in her capacity as freelance editor and hired gun.

It is not surprising that a town as beautiful as Macon has given rise to a large number of pictorial histories, and a quick glance at the bibliography will reveal that we are not alone in this endeavor. We hope our contribution to this rich field lies in our book's chronological scope and inclusivity—from first peoples to the early 21st century with an eye toward demonstrating Macon's shared, and tortured, racial history.

Our families and friends played crucial roles in shaping this work, and we owe deep debts of gratitude to the many people who support our academic endeavors. In the end, though, since we began to think of this book as part of a larger project to do justice to Macon's past, we decided to dedicate the book to the people of Macon—past, present, and future.

INTRODUCTION

Macon. The name itself can call to mind myriad images depending on the time period being remembered and the person doing the recollecting. For some, Macon means gracious antebellum homes, relaxed living, and the attendant Southern hospitality; for others, Macon means grinding poverty. At the same time, the city's history points toward hope against lingering oppression and beauty in the struggle for human dignity—both memories are accurate and true. Both of these Macons—and many more besides—have existed for a very long time.

The chance to put together a pictorial history of Macon was too great an opportunity to pass up, even if the authors cannot claim ancestral Maconite status. We are lifelong students of history, and this is our meager attempt to tell the story of the community we both call home using visual evidence from multiple centuries. It is not a full reckoning of Macon's past; while such a work is sorely needed, it is beyond the scope of the Images of America series. Including every historic home, lauding every denomination and congregation, and name-checking every famous personage would require a much lengthier book. Our effort is, by its very nature, incomplete. We have chosen images we found compelling and have sought to use these images to convey what we believe to be the major themes of Macon's history.

One of those themes is race relations. After studying the city's history and observing recent political developments, it is impossible for us to discuss Macon without calling attention to the racial divide that has cut through much of that history. Even in the early 21st century, the line between blacks and whites persists, albeit as more of an "unutterable separation" than the strict segregation of earlier decades.

An equally persistent theme has been economic development. In the earliest editions of the *Telegraph*, Macon's longtime newspaper, readers can find evidence of the belief that the city's good times are ever on the horizon, and the next big project will launch the town into a wonderland of prosperity. Macon has been around long enough to experience several heydays, as well as several rough patches.

The book begins with the Ocmulgee River and flows through Macon's history in a series of chronological chapters from the region's earliest occupation (at present-day Ocmulgee National Monument) through the rise of the cotton economy and slavery. Among Macon's most famous landmarks are the Cannonball House, where one shot was fired during the Civil War, and the Johnson-Felton-Hay House, an ornate mansion completed just as the Civil War began. The large number of antebellum buildings that still stand in the city might cause a casual visitor to conclude that Macon was essentially untouched by the war, but a closer examination reveals a different story.

Civil War–era Macon bustled with activity. Unlike many Southern cities, Macon already possessed a significant industrial economy, and that economy was quickly put to work in the service of the Confederate cause. Troops and supplies traveled via the Macon & Western Railroad to support the Army of the Tennessee as Union troops marched south from Chattanooga to lay siege to Atlanta. Macon provided the primary hospital facilities for Confederate troops driven out of Atlanta. Captured Union officers waited out the war, often in miserable conditions, at Camp Oglethorpe. While Macon saw very little actual combat, significant battles took place in the surrounding areas, and Macon's role as a support and logistics center was crucial to the last-ditch Confederate efforts to stave off Union general William T. Sherman's ustoppable March to the Sea.

Macon's Findlay Iron Works housed the Confederate States Arsenal, which produced cannon tubes and carriages as well as "shoes, saddles, shells . . . revolving pistols, knapsacks, cartridge box belts, Columbiad carriages from oak timber, and flannel for cartridge bags," according to historian Richard W. Iobst. Macon's Confederate Armory, located a few blocks away, also manufactured pistols, rifle barrels, and as many as 1,500 gun stocks per month. Downtown Macon also housed a research facility, the Confederate States Laboratory, that contributed to the growing standardization of ammunition through the efforts of Irish chemist John W. Mallet.

The Civil War legacy remained a crucial feature of Macon's identity long after the shooting stopped. Like many Southern cities and towns, Macon made a great effort to commemorate the war, erecting monuments and hosting reunions for decades after the fight ended. Though the Civil War destroyed slavery, cotton agriculture and textile mills remained significant well into the 20th century, and the racist caste system survived even longer. In the 20th century, Macon witnessed multiple periods of dramatic growth and cultural flowering, even as black Maconites struggled for meaningful equality in the face of massive white resistance. In more recent years, the decline of manufacturing exacted a heavy toll, and the town nearly drowned in the flood of 1994. Today, booming health care and education sectors, tourist dollars, and even a nascent film industry are breathing new life into Macon.

Macon has plenty of nicknames, but "City of Churches" is among the most apt. Throughout Macon's history, the faithful have gathered in hundreds of different sites around town, and these houses of worship reflect Macon's dynamic and diverse religious heritage. In addition to select religious architecture throughout the book, we thought it appropriate to close with a chapter that speaks directly to the faith of Macon's people and to how that faith has both persisted and evolved over time.

There is pain in Macon's story, but there is pride in equal measure. There is deep prejudice, but dignity and defiance also have leading roles. We hope Macon sees something of itself in this slim volume, and we hope that it may play some small part in our adopted hometown's struggle to confront, celebrate, and make sense of its past.

One

ANCIENT GRANDEUR
MACON'S FIRST MONUMENTS

Macon's history begins with a river. The Ocmulgee River has been Central Georgia's lifeline for millennia. The first people to live in Middle Georgia occupied seasonal hunting camps near the river. Over time, Native American civilizations, including those called "Mississippians" by later scholars, mastered the rich environment near the floodplain. Between 950 and 1050 AD, the people who lived along the Ocmulgee River built the monumental earthworks that tower over the area today. Five hundred years later and a few miles downriver, Hernando de Soto's army visited the town of Ichisi when it passed through the region in 1540.

Native communities weathered the storm of several waves of Spanish adventurers. By the time English colonists established Carolina in the late 17th century, native people were familiar with Europeans, as well as the benefits and drawbacks of forging a relationship with them. From 1690 to 1715, the banks of the Ocmulgee hummed with activity as the English established a trading post in the shadow of the Great Temple Mound. Natives from throughout the region moved to the banks of the river the English called "Ocheesse Creek," where they could exchange deerskins and captives for guns, horses, hatchets, and other goods. The violence of Carolina's Yamasee War spilled into the frontier, forcing the abandonment of the trading post, but the "Creek" name given by the English stuck, and the Creeks and English continued to trade and interact in other ways. The Ocmulgee town sites continued to serve as important way stations on the Creek trading path from Charles Town, on the Carolina coast, to the Chattahoochee River in the west.

After the Revolutionary War, the permanent settler presence and the insatiable land hunger that accompanied it put heavy pressure on the Creek Nation. The Creeks were forced to surrender the land that would become Macon through a series of treaties culminating in the Treaty of Washington in 1826. That treaty, and others like it, began the tragic removal and relocation of Native Americans known as "The Trail of Tears."

The Ocmulgee River forms when the Yellow, Alcovy, and South Rivers converge in north central Georgia. Just above Macon, the Ocmulgee crosses the fall line and becomes navigable. After passing through Macon, it flows nearly 200 miles before joining with the Oconee River to form the Altamaha, which in turn empties into the Atlantic Ocean near present-day Darien, Georgia. The river ensured that exchange of people, goods, and ideas would be a hallmark of Macon's development from the first dugout canoes to the age of cotton. (Photograph by Matthew Jennings.)

The area near the floodplain of the Ocmulgee River has been the site of continuous human occupation for as long as 17,000 years. The combination of the floodplain and the fall line engendered a particularly rich mix of plant and animal life. Around 1000 AD, members of what archaeologists term the Mississippian culture built a central plaza, several earthworks, a distinctive council house, and homes for hundreds of families. The Mississippian town site (now known as Ocmulgee) lies just across the river from present-day downtown Macon. (National Park Service, Ocmulgee National Monument.)

The plaza was the center of any Mississippian town, and many plazas predate their surrounding earthworks. Plazas were key gathering places at ceremonially significant times of the year (such as during the Green Corn celebration that occurred each summer and honored the renewal of the world), and they were also used as venues for sporting contests. (National Park Service, Ocmulgee National Monument.)

Historians and archaeologists identify Mississippian cultures in part by their towns, which contained massive earthworks. This 1970 photograph shows the Great and Lesser Temple Mounds. The Great Temple Mound, built around 1000 AD, rises to a height of 55 feet, accentuating the natural rise in the landscape. The Lesser Temple Mound suffered severe damage due to railroad construction in the 1840s. Platform mounds, or truncated pyramids, were home to Mississippian civil and religious leaders, who reportedly drew their power from a close connection to the sun. (National Park Service, Ocmulgee National Monument.)

Many Mississippian sites featured platform mounds, though few are as well preserved as those at Ocmulgee. Council houses are much rarer, and Ocmulgee's is particularly beautiful. In a misguided attempt to preserve it, the council house was capped with a concrete dome and covered with turf in the 1930s (hence the misnomer "Earth Lodge"), but the floor is original and is approximately 1,000 years old. (National Park Service, Ocmulgee National Monument.)

The floor of the council house, which is a nearly perfect circle, features a raised platform in the shape a bird of prey, perhaps an eagle or falcon. Southeastern Native Americans revered birds of prey for their daring. Twice each year, the sun shone through the entrance passage directly onto the highest seat on the platform, suggesting a connection between leadership and the sun. (National Park Service, Ocmulgee National Monument.)

A town the size of Ocmulgee (the population was likely in the low thousands) required a complicated system of governance. Certain lineages produced civil, military, and religious leaders, and while there was probably a single leader, he rarely made any significant decisions without consulting advisors. Ned Jenkins built this diorama and many others for the National Park Service in the late 1940s. (National Park Service, Ocmulgee National Monument.)

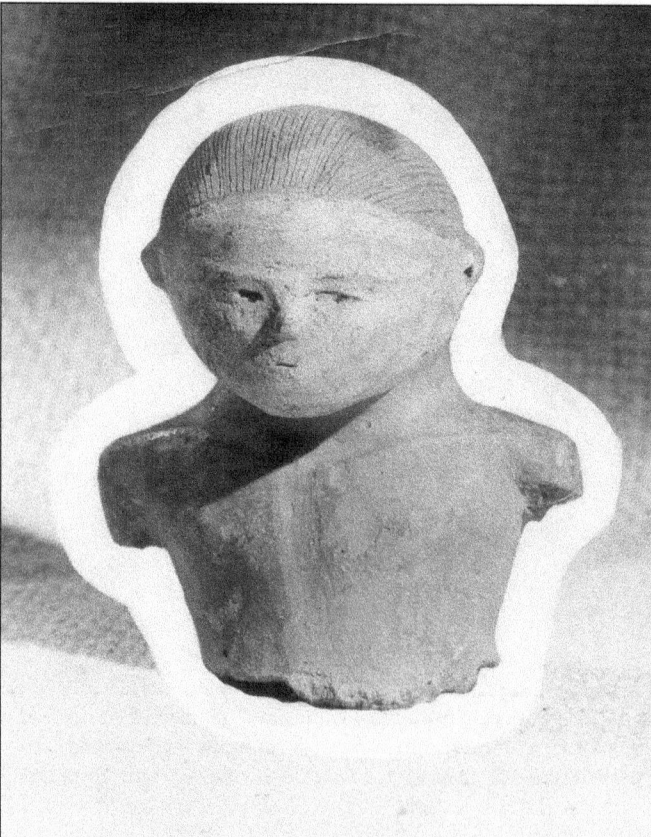

Mississippians fashioned elaborate items from clay, and archaeologists have unearthed thousands of pieces from the Macon area. Pieces like this were formed by smoothing coils of clay and then stamping on the pattern with a wooden paddle. (National Park Service, Ocmulgee National Monument.)

This piece, dubbed "Little Man," was likely a finely made bottle-stopper or an effigy of a young child. (National Park Service, Ocmulgee National Monument.)

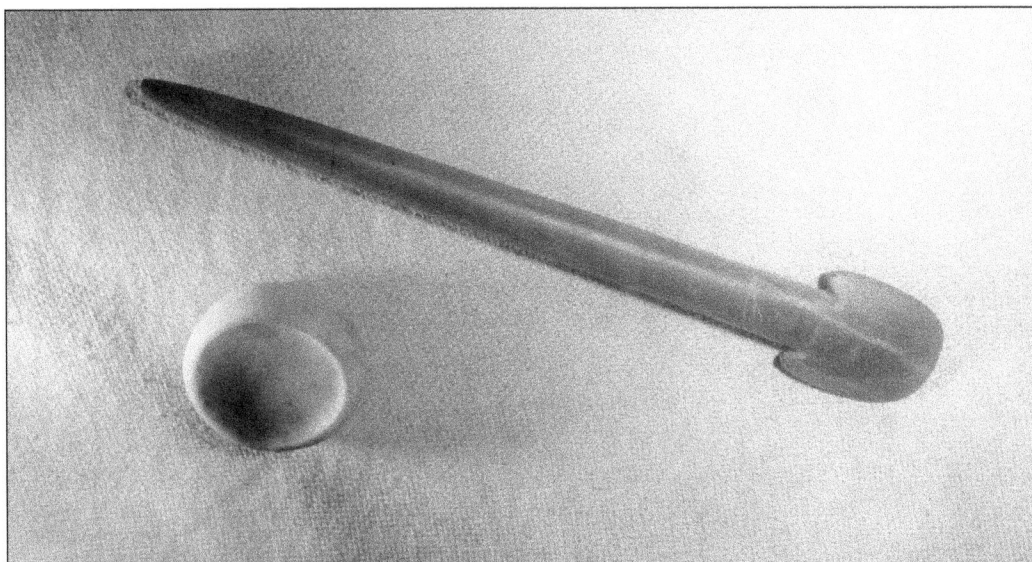

Throughout the Mississippian time period, native people played a game called "chunkey." Someone rolled a smooth stone disk out into the central plaza, and young men would compete by throwing spears or shooting arrows to predict where the stone would stop. Chunkey provided training for warfare and an opportunity for community-wide recreational gambling. Also pictured is a stone axe known as a celt. (National Park Service, Ocmulgee National Monument.)

The agricultural world of the Mississippians was fairly diverse. They hunted and ate wild foods such as berries and herbs, but they also cultivated corn, beans, squash, and tobacco. They smoked tobacco during rituals using specially made pipes such as this elegant bird-shaped device. (National Park Service, Ocmulgee National Monument.)

In the middle of the 20th century, archaeologists used the phrase "Master Farmer" to denote the Mississippians and created this model to display reconstructed versions of some of the artifacts found at Ocmulgee. Note the stone celt in the model's hand and the elaborate headdress fashioned from panthers' jaws and copper disks reminiscent of the rays of the sun or a seashell. (National Park Service, Ocmulgee National Monument.)

While the large town at Ocmulgee was essentially abandoned by 1200, another Mississippian town sprang up slightly downriver. Archaeologists called this Lamar for the family that owned the land in the 19th century. It is likely that this was the town of "Ichisi" mentioned in the documents of the Hernando de Soto expedition (which took place from 1539 to 1543). In addition to a square platform mound, Lamar features a spiral mound with a ramp winding its way to the top. Relations between Ichisi and the Spanish were benign compared to the havoc wrought elsewhere by de Soto's army. (National Park Service, Ocmulgee National Monument.)

In the 17th century, the Ocmulgee area was transformed again by the eastward migration of Muskogean-speaking people from the Chattahoochee River country along what is now the Alabama-Georgia border. The Ocmulgee site provided an ideal location for natives to trade with the English without getting too close to the main English settlement at Charles Town. Muskogees, and other peoples who eventually formed the Creek Nation, forged a tenuous but profitable alliance with the English. The arrangement did not work out particularly well for the natives of Spanish Florida. This diorama shows an early-18th-century raid, one of several that resulted in the seizure of thousands of captives. (National Park Service, Ocmulgee National Monument.)

Philadelphia naturalist William Bartram, who visited the Ocmulgee area in the 1770s and commented on the ancient mounds and fields, sketched a Creek public square in the 1790s; that sketch formed the basis of this diorama. The square grounds at the center of Creek towns echo the Mississippian-era plazas. (National Park Service, Ocmulgee National Monument.)

Fort Hawkins, Macon, Ga.

Pres. Thomas Jefferson authorized the construction of Fort Benjamin Hawkins in 1806 to advance federal interests in Creek country and protect what was then the southern border of the United States. For more than a decade, the fort served as a trading post. (Matthew Jennings.)

Two

COTTON, SLAVERY, AND CIVIL WAR
THE BIRTH OF MACON

As Fort Hawkins outlived its usefulness, a small settlement called Newtown arose on the east side of the Ocmulgee. In 1823, the first lots on the west side of the river were put up for auction, signaling the beginning of Macon (the town was named for Nathaniel Macon, an influential North Carolina legislator). From Macon's establishment—and continuing through most of its first century—the town's fortunes rose and fell with cotton. Innovations in the late 18th century sparked the proliferation of short staple cotton through a wide swath of the Southeastern United States. Thanks to steamboat and railroad trade, Macon became a center of cotton commerce. Steamboat service connected Macon to Darien and the coast, and the Central of Georgia Railway linked Macon to Savannah.

Chattel slavery, the labor regime that produced cotton wealth, was an abomination that kept African Americans locked in generational servitude and perpetual fear of violence and separation from loved ones. In spite of this, enslaved men and women proved their humanity again and again by forging a community based in resistance and by running away against tremendous odds. Slaves on the plantations surrounding Macon labored primarily in cotton fields, but within the city itself, slaves performed nearly every kind of work imaginable. According to the 1860 census, just over one-third of the town's 8,200 residents were enslaved. The city itself owned slaves and put them to work cleaning and maintaining the streets. Cotton agriculture secured Macon's economic development in the years prior to the Civil War but at a terrible human cost. Some of Macon's architectural gems date from the antebellum period, and some of its most compelling characters, including Ellen and William Craft, made their names in the same era.

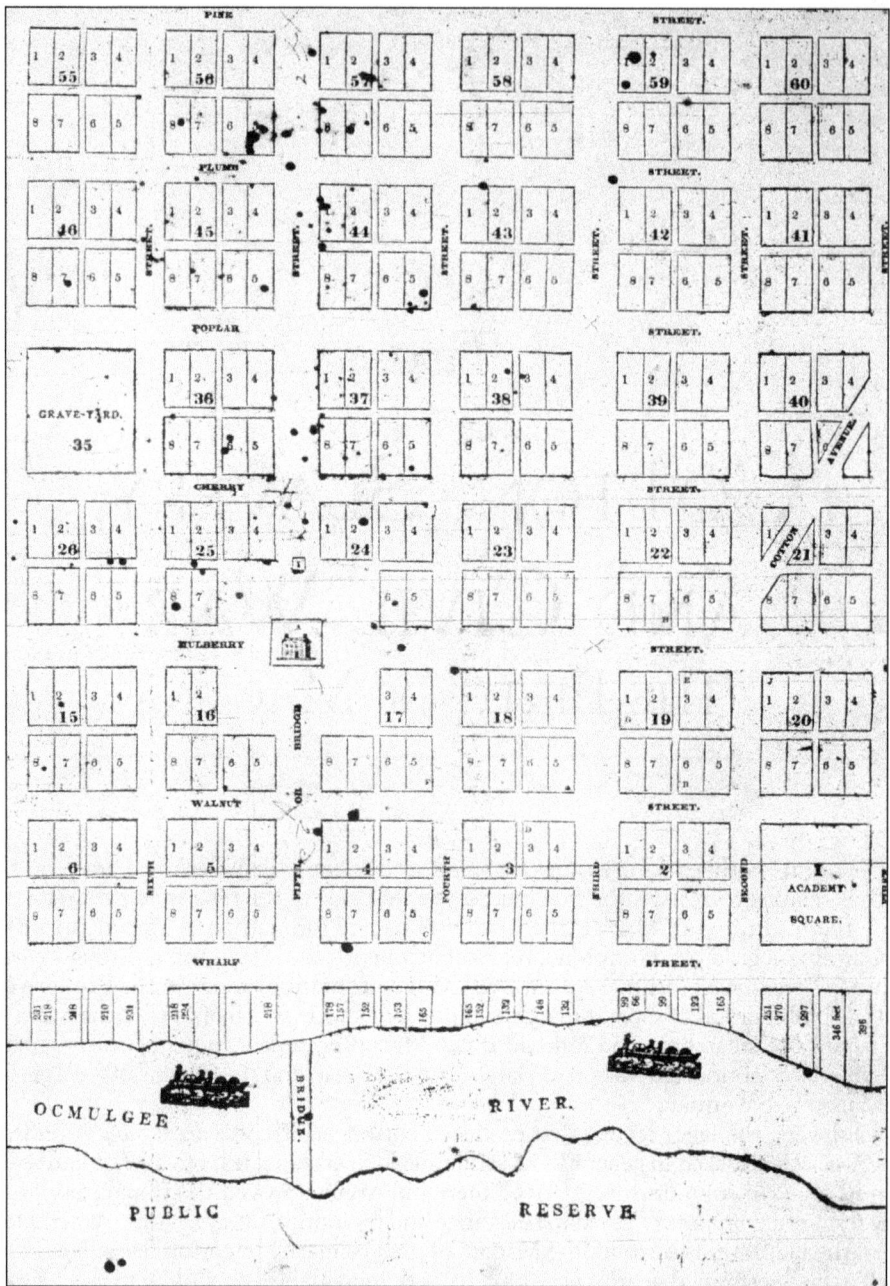

The Macon *Telegraph Advertiser*, then a weekly paper, published this map in July 1831. The original plan has remained hugely influential ever since, though Wharf Street is now known as Riverside Drive. Note the spaces set aside for a graveyard, an academy, and a courthouse. Cotton Avenue, which runs at an angle to the grid, was Macon's section of the already-extant federal road through the area. Prominent Maconites insisted on wide streets (these alternate between widths of 120 and 180 feet) and public land to preserve health and the robust natural environment. It is also clear from the stylized steamboats on the river that the planners envisioned a prosperous future linked to river trade. The text accompanying the map notes that "In morals, there is no *new* town that can boast of more refinement." (Middle Georgia Archives, Washington Memorial Library.)

John Gresham had this mansion built in 1842. Gresham, a wealthy attorney, cotton merchant, and judge, was mayor of Macon twice in the 1840s. In 1900, B.F. Adams purchased the property and undertook substantial renovations that made the building the Greek Revival masterpiece it is today. Currently, the building houses a hotel known as the 1842 Inn. (Photograph by David Jennings.)

The Andrews House, located at 110 Third Street (the corner of Third and Wharf Streets), was built for Lewis F.W. Andrews and his wife, Jane, beginning in 1856. The Bibb County deed book notes that the Andrews family sold the house in 1860 for $7,000. (Library of Congress, Historic American Buildings Survey.)

This home was built in 1830 for Ambrose Baber, Macon's first practicing physician. Baber, in addition to practicing medicine, served in the military in the War of 1812 and in the diplomatic corps in the John Tyler administration. Baber died in 1846 as a result of a strange accidental poisoning. In addition to its time as a private residence, this building has also served as a hospital and now houses a law firm. (Library of Congress, Historic American Buildings Survey.)

The first courthouse in Macon was built in 1829 and, in accordance with the original town plan, stood on a square where Fifth Street met Mulberry Street. The lead architect on the project was Elam Alexander, who designed several of Macon's most important early buildings. In the 1870s, the county government moved to Second and Mulberry Streets, where it remains today. The nearby Macon Gas Light Company opened in 1853. (Middle Georgia Archives, Washington Memorial Library.)

Elam Alexander designed this mansion at 1129 Georgia Avenue for Judge Thaddeus Goode Holt between 1830 and 1840. Judge Holt was among the prominent citizens who escorted the Marquis de Lafayette into Macon during the Marquis's 1825 visit. Holt was a Unionist in the 1850s, though he eventually supported secession. (David Jennings.)

Elam Alexander started work on this Greek Revival mansion in 1836 at the request of Jerry Cowles. When financial disaster befell Cowles in 1847, Joseph Bond bought the estate. Bond, among Georgia's wealthiest residents at the time, ran seven plantations worked by 1,300 slaves. An overseer shot and killed Bond in an 1859 dispute. More recently, in 1960, white parents upset by the prospect of integration used this building to house Stratford Academy. This house is now owned by Mercer University and serves as a beautiful special events center. (Photograph by Matthew Jennings.)

Cadwalader (also known as Cadwell) Raines built this home at 1183 Georgia Avenue in 1846. Raines was president of the Central Georgia Bank at the time. The house features a distinctive spiral staircase that ascends from the entrance hall to the cupola. (Library of Congress, Historic American Buildings Survey.)

The Greek Revival home at 856 Mulberry Street (pictured at right) is known as the Cannonball House. Judge Asa Holt ordered the house built at a cost of $7,000 in 1853. In addition to serving as a judge, Holt owned a 1,500-acre plantation in Jefferson County. In 1864, during the battle of Dunlap Hill, the house was struck by a Union artillery shell. The Holt family owned the house until the 1970s, when they deeded it to the local chapter of the United Daughters of the Confederacy. Because of this, and owing to the fact that the house was one of the very few in Macon damaged by the Union army, the house has been a central site for retaining Confederate memories. Interestingly, the site contains a crucial element of Macon's black history, too. The building below, which housed the kitchen and slave quarters, is one of a handful of urban slave quarters still standing in Georgia. (Right, Library of Congress, Historic American Buildings Survey; below, photograph by Matthew Jennings.)

This 1851 photograph taken on Cotton Avenue is notable for a couple of reasons: first, its date makes it one of the earliest photographic images of Macon; second, apart from the carriage maker, the photograph shows a Daguerrian gallery. Daguerreotype was the first widely available form of modern photography. (Middle Georgia Archives, Washington Memorial Library.)

This building, also designed by Elam Alexander, housed the Bibb County Academy (formerly the Female Academy) from 1844 to 1864. Merrel P. Callaway owned the structure from 1865 to 1895, after which the Macon Hospital Association bought it. (Library of Congress, Historic American Buildings Survey.)

PICKING COTTON ON A GEORGIA PLANTATION.

Cotton-picking was among the most degrading, depressing forms of slavery, but one would not know that from the way the institution was depicted in many publications. The 1858 engraving shown above, "Picking Cotton on a Georgia Plantation," from *Ballou's Pictorial*, shows happy, well-clothed, and well-fed slaves picking cotton. The remembrances of slaves are at odds with this portrayal. Solomon Northup, a free man captured and held as a slave, described the violence at the heart of the system in his memoir *Twelve Years a Slave*: "When a new hand, one unaccustomed to the business, is sent for the first time into the field, he is whipped up smartly, and made for that day to pick as fast as he can possibly." After weighing the cotton, slaves were expected to maintain that pace of production, or "it is considered evidence that he has been laggard, and a greater or less number of lashes is the penalty." The image below is a stereoscope depicting cotton agriculture. (Both, Library of Congress.)

Ellen and William Craft were skilled slaves when they met in Macon in the 1840s. William was a carpenter and Ellen a seamstress. Urban slavery allowed somewhat more autonomy than plantation slavery, and urban slaves could occasionally work for wages, provided they returned those wages to their owners. Ellen and William planned to set themselves free and used their wages to accumulate a bizarre disguise for Ellen. She would pose as a sickly white man heading north to seek medical treatment, and William would accompany her while pretending to be her slave. (Engraving from William Still, *The Underground Railroad*, 1872.)

Though they barely escaped detection while waiting for the train to pull out of Macon, their plan worked. The two married in Boston before living in England for more than a decade. They told their daring story in *Running a Thousand Miles for Freedom*, published in 1860. Just a few years after the escape, Ellen wrote that "I had much rather starve in England, a free woman, than be a slave for the best man that ever breathed upon the American continent." (Engraving from William Still, *The Underground Railroad*, 1872.)

J.S. Schofield founded this ironworks in 1850, though the building pictured above dates to the end of the 1850s. Schofield produced a variety of machinery, much of it tied to plantation agriculture. During the Civil War, much of Schofield's production was used toward military purposes. Eventually, Taylor Iron took over the ironworks. Taylor remained in business until the 1970s. (Both, Middle Georgia Archives, Washington Memorial Library.)

Though cotton agriculture was the most important economic activity around Macon, the city itself was not bereft of industrial development. In 1838, Scottish-born Robert Findlay arrived in Macon. By 1854, he had bought out various partners and was the proprietor of Findlay Iron Works, with operations in Atlanta and Griffin, and had built over 100 stationary steam engines, including this 1852 model. Findlay died in 1859, but his ironworks survived until 1912. (Middle Georgia Archives, Washington Memorial Library.)

The First Presbyterian Church, located at 852 Mulberry Street, was established as a congregation in 1826—soon after Macon's founding. This building was consecrated in 1858. The church counted poet Sidney Lanier among its members. The building itself is remarkable for the height of its steeple. The 185-foot-tall structure towered over Macon and was the tallest building in town from 1858 until St. Joseph Catholic Church was finished in 1903. (Library of Congress, Historic American Buildings Survey.)

Though this house is often referred to as the Hay House (in honor of its last private owner), construction began on it in 1855 at the request of William Johnston. Johnston, a merchant and banker, hired New York–based architects T. Thomas and Son to design the mansion in an Italianate style. It contained 24 rooms, central heating, and indoor plumbing, which was quite rare at the time. During the Civil War, Johnston served as the head of the Confederate States of America depository, leading to rumors that huge amounts of Confederate gold were squirreled away in the residence. To call the interior lavish would be an understatement, as Johnson and subsequent owners spared no expense on decor. The Georgia Trust for Historic Preservation inherited the house in 1977 and has managed it ever since; it is one of Middle Georgia's most recognizable landmarks. (Both, Library of Congress, Historic American Buildings Survey.)

Macon's city hall was not originally intended to be a government building; it was built as the bank run by the Monroe Railroad in the 1830s. When that railroad failed, Jerry Cowles bought the building. It served as a warehouse and briefly functioned as the state capitol during the Civil War. This photograph shows city hall as it appeared in 1894. (Middle Georgia Archives, Washington Memorial Library.)

Frenchman Mathuren Arthur Andrieu painted this Mulberry Street scene in 1851. At right, one can see the Mulberry Methodist Church (and the Bond/Woodruff House in the distance). The left side shows a parade of the Macon Volunteers. The Macon Guard, formed from the ranks of the Volunteers, marched alongside regular US Army forces during the invasion of Mexico in 1846. Capt. Isaac Holmes, who was mayor at the time, died in Camp Monterey in December of that year. (Middle Georgia Archives, Washington Memorial Library.)

The first colonists in Middle Georgia buried their dead in the cemetery next to Fort Hawkins, sometimes known as Fort Hill Cemetery. The 1820s plan for Macon set aside a site on Cherry Street for a graveyard, the remnants of which are still around today. In 1840, at the urging of Simri Rose, Macon wholeheartedly joined the "rural cemetery" movement when it built Rose Hill Cemetery (pictured above in 1894) overlooking the Ocmulgee. Cemeteries were no longer drab, overgrown burying grounds but rather places of repose where families could visit their departed loved ones. The Oak Ridge Cemetery, founded the same year and pictured below, held the remains of enslaved men and women owned by Macon's wealthiest families. (Above, Middle Georgia Archives, Washington Memorial Library; below, photograph by Matthew Jennings.)

The early 19th century was a fairly chaotic time in the banking industry, and the federal government offered a minimal stabilizing influence. Individual banks issued their own notes more or less as they chose. This particular note is a $5 bill from the Ocmulgee Bank. The design includes a romanticized Native American, a steamboat, a wagon loaded with cotton, and what appears to be a plantation mistress. (Matthew Jennings.)

Throughout most of the 19th century, Macon's Poplar Street was the place to buy and sell every Saturday. Shops lined the street, but commerce also took place in the wide middle of the thoroughfare. Although this scene is from a slightly later time period, it captures the spirit of the market. In the antebellum period, enslaved women were among the leading marketeers who sold produce from their families' gardens. Poplar Street was also the center of Macon's slave trade, and several slave dealers had shops on Poplar. (Middle Georgia Archives, Washington Memorial Library.)

34

By the 1840s (the time represented in this drawing), Macon was linked to several other towns by rail. The Monroe Railroad (later known as the Macon & Western) ran between Macon and Forsyth. This eventually became part of the Georgia Railroad, which connected to Marthasville (later known as Atlanta) in 1845. To the east, Macon was connected to Savannah and the coast by the Central of Georgia Railway, which ran 190 miles across the coastal plain. The grading for the Central of Georgia, completed mainly by slaves rented from surrounding plantations, did irreparable damage to several key archaeological sites at Ocmulgee. (Middle Georgia Archives, Washington Memorial Library.)

The steamship bell pictured on this postcard is believed to have rung on one of the first ships to make the run from Macon down to Darien via the Ocmulgee and Altamaha Rivers. The bell from the riverboat *Ocmulgee* was a gift from Maj. John Cobb to Macon mayor Bridges Smith in 1900. For years, the bell sat in the triangular park formed by Cotton Avenue and Second Street, but it eventually made its way to Central City Park. (Marsha Brockman.)

Southern Botanico-Medical College was a private medical school that opened on Mulberry Street in the 1840s and operated for about 40 years. As one might gather from the name, the instructors there taught pupils plant-based remedies for ailments and generally practiced reform medicine as opposed to hydropathy or other 19th-century medical schools of thought. (Middle Georgia Archives, Washington Memorial Library.)

Wesleyan College, which was chartered in 1836 as the Georgia Female College, holds the distinction of being the oldest women's college in the United States. The college opened its doors in 1839 and had 90 students at the time. The building pictured here no longer stands on College Street up the hill from Washington Park, and in the 1920s, Wesleyan moved to the suburban village of Rivoli, which itself was later absorbed into Macon. (Middle Georgia Archives, Washington Memorial Library.)

Jefferson Long was born a slave in Alabama in 1836. Before the Civil War, he worked as a tailor in Macon, and he also learned to read and write by assisting with typesetting at a nearby newspaper. Freed by the general emancipation at the end of the Civil War, Long went to work for himself and was drawn to Republican party politics along with other AME Church members, including Henry McNeal Turner. Long was elected to the US House of Representatives in 1870, during Reconstruction, and gave a speech denouncing the racist violence then gripping the South. The reinstatement of white supremacy and Democratic rule in Georgia politics ended his tenure in Congress. He returned to Macon, attempted to organize black voters in the face of limited options, and operated a successful dry cleaning business. Long died in 1901 and is buried in Linwood Cemetery. (Right, Library of Congress; below, photograph by Matthew Jennings.)

UNITED STATES CONGRESSMAN
A MEMBER OF THE HOUSE OF REPRESENTATIVES
41ST CONGRESS
1870 — 1871
JEFFERSON FRANKLIN LONG
COMMONLY KNOWN AS
"JEFF LONG"
MARCH 3, 1836 — FEBRUARY 4, 1901

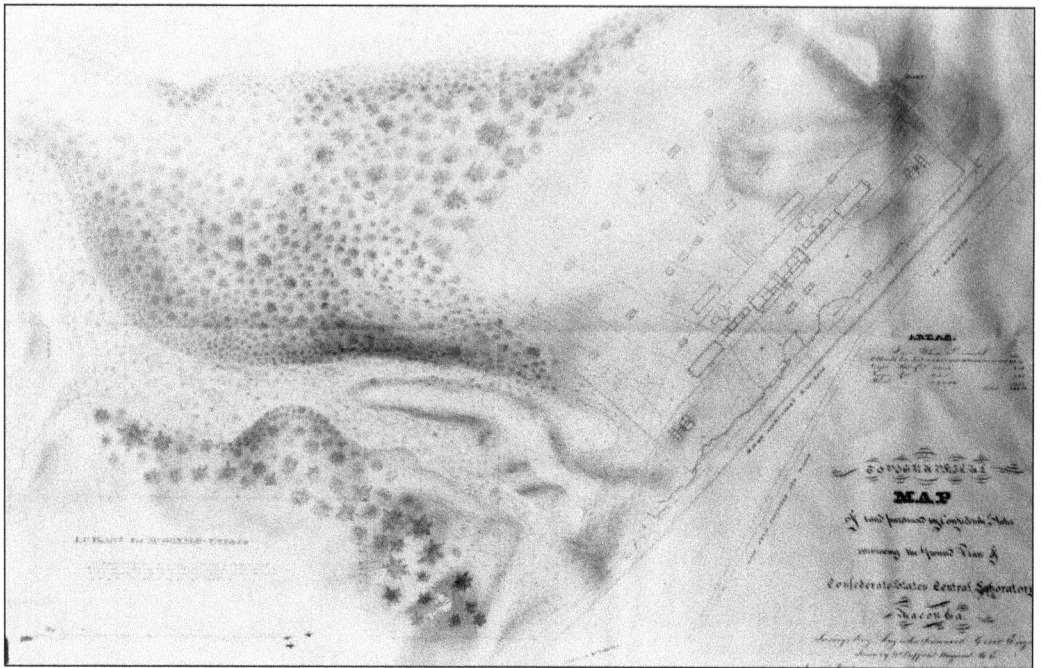

This sketch shows the original site plan for the Confederate States Laboratory, where experiments determined appropriate dimensions for ammunition as well as the optimum powder charge to use for each type of weapon. (Middle Georgia Archives, Washington Memorial Library.)

CONFEDERATE STATES LABORATORY—BUILT IN 1862

This is the Confederate States Laboratory main building as it appeared after the Civil War. (Middle Georgia Archives, Washington Memorial Library.)

Parts of the Confederate States Laboratory were never finished, and by 1915, the structure was on the verge of collapse. (Middle Georgia Archives, Washington Memorial Library.)

This "market scene" of downtown Macon dramatizes the extent to which the end of slavery brought new people to the city in the years immediately after the Civil War. (Middle Georgia Archives, Washington Memorial Library.)

JEFFERSON DAVIS A PRISONER
PASSING THROUGH MACON, GEORGIA, IN AN AMBULANCE

After Confederate president Jefferson Davis was captured, he traveled through Macon in a horse-drawn ambulance as crowds gathered to show either respect or disappointment. (Middle Georgia Archives, Washington Memorial Library.)

Poet Sidney Lanier was born in 1842 in this house, which belonged to his grandparents. He graduated from, and briefly taught at, Oglethorpe College in Milledgeville before entering the Macon Volunteers and the Confederate army in 1861. During the war, he was captured on a blockade runner and spent five months in federal prison. Lanier was an extremely versatile and talented man. Though best known as a poet (he wrote "The Marshes of Glynn" in 1878 and taught English literature at Johns Hopkins), he was also an accomplished musician, mathematician, and linguist. (Photograph by Matthew Jennings.)

Three

RISE, FALL, AND RISE
BUSINESS AND INDUSTRY
IN MACON'S GOLDEN AGE

In the 1870s and 1880s, Atlanta newspaper editor Henry Grady exhorted Southerners to diversify their economic base and move beyond their dependence on cotton agriculture. Macon, already more industrialized than many Southern communities, built on that foundation with textile manufacturing, transportation, retail, and other businesses.

A series of economic difficulties began with the panic of 1893. Those who had staked their entire futures on industrialization found that there were few resources to fall back on. With no cash income, they could not purchase necessities, and with little land, they could not feed themselves. A generation later, the even more severe economic downturn known as the Great Depression fundamentally transformed the American landscape as people moved from farms beset by boll weevils to towns where, if there was no work right away, at least there was hope for work at some future date.

The federal response to the Great Depression, the New Deal, brought new opportunities and new complications. Government programs provided both temporary relief and long-term restructuring to the American economy, and Macon's citizens—black and white—responded. World War II brought Americans of all backgrounds together against a common enemy, though they were often still physically kept apart from each other.

Through all this dislocation and upheaval, Macon remained a vital—if not always thriving—community, and the optimism of its residents fueled continuing efforts to move forward.

ecard St looking South west from Bibb court House

This view of downtown Macon clearly shows the multitude of cables necessary to carry direct electric current. The switch to alternating current a few years later allowed for a much cleaner view. (Middle Georgia Archives, Washington Memorial Library.)

The F.M. Haygood store, pictured here in 1875, typified post–Civil War stores that sold some of everything. Haygood sold books, music, and sewing machines—and one wonders what else the store contained. (Middle Georgia Archives, Washington Memorial Library.)

Naming a business after the South was a sure way to the hearts of Macon's white customers. Above is a c. 1900 photograph of the Dixie Company. Despite sectional loyalty, it was difficult for Dixie Company to compete with the impressive array of goods available at Union Dry Goods Company, pictured below at night. (Both, Middle Georgia Archives, Washington Memorial Library.)

Transportation was always a lucrative business for a savvy owner. The Collins and Little Carriage Company, located on Cherry Street, is pictured at left around 1875. By 1910, market forces had pressed the Coleman Buggy Company to diversify its offerings, as indicated by the automobile for sale in the front of the building. (Both, Middle Georgia Archives, Washington Memorial Library.)

In the 1870s, Henry Grady advised the South to invest in industries that had little or no connection to cotton. By the 1890s, Macon residents had opened both the Acme Brewery (above) and the Macon Brewing Company (below). As of 2013, a group of investors announced that they had obtained the rights to brew beer again in Macon under the Macon Beer Company name. (Both, Middle Georgia Archives, Washington Memorial Library.)

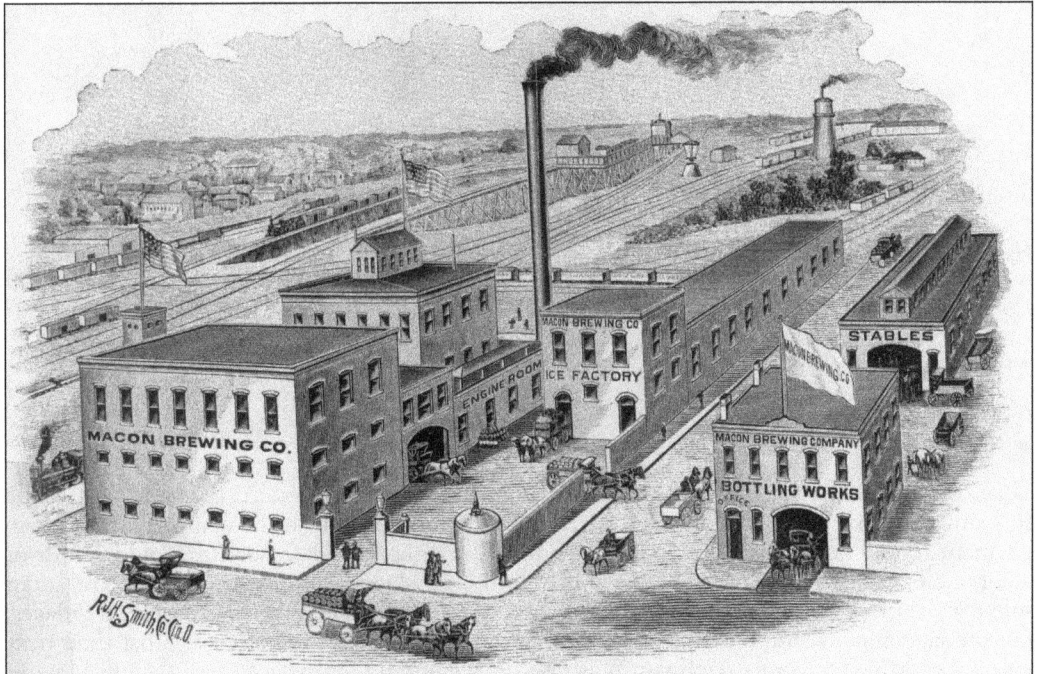

As late as 1915, despite the arrival of the automobile, W.G. Lee earned a significant profit dealing in horses and mules, as suggested by this picture. (Middle Georgia Archives, Washington Memorial Library.)

In many company towns, employees were paid in scrip redeemable at the company store. Scrip payments could not be used for goods the employers disapproved of, such as playing cards or alcoholic beverages. "Cash stores" like this one in East Macon did not accept scrip and often sold a wider array of goods at lower prices than company-owned enterprises in the mill villages, but unlike company stores, cash stores would not allow employees to borrow against their next paycheck. (Middle Georgia Archives, Washington Memorial Library.)

Though diversification was the key to long-term economic growth, Macon's proximity to agricultural areas made it a natural location for textile mills that often processed cotton grown only a few miles away. Above, the Campbell & Jones Cotton Factory Warehouse on Poplar Street is shown in 1887. Below, the Atlantic Cotton Mill is shown in a 1925 photograph. The Atlantic Cotton Mill building, located just off Pio Nono Avenue, was slated for redevelopment until a fire destroyed it in 2012. (Both, Middle Georgia Archives, Washington Memorial Library.)

The mill shown above was one of several properties owned by the Bibb Manufacturing Company. Below is a portrait of a group of workers at the same mill. Throughout most of the South until World War II, most industrial jobs were reserved for white workers, with exceptions made only for the dirtiest or most dangerous work. (Both, Middle Georgia Archives, Washington Memorial Library.)

The ability to join the growing urban middle class required an education. The St. Joseph Catholic Church sponsored this school (pictured in the 1880s) on Fourth Street. (Middle Georgia Archives, Washington Memorial Library.)

Downtown businesses such as the Campbell T. King Drugstore on Cotton Avenue could count on a steady supply of customers from the rapidly growing urban population. (Middle Georgia Archives, Washington Memorial Library.)

By the end of the 19th century, Macon's businesses responded to the growing sophistication of their customers by offering more and better merchandise. The Dannenberg Company is pictured above in 1900. The Haskins Department Store on Poplar Street is pictured below in 1912. (Both, Middle Georgia Archives, Washington Memorial Library.)

For those with means enough to display, fashion was very important as a means of distinguishing the up-and-coming entrepreneur, attorney, or accountant from his neighbor. Fine goods at equally fine prices could be purchased from merchants such as Philip M. Berg (right) or Joseph E. Neel (below), both of whom dealt in gentlemen's apparel. (Both, Middle Georgia Archives, Washington Memorial Library.)

As mass production took over from independent producers, Macon merchants had to grow and change. S.S. Parmalee, whose business is pictured above, sold quality carriages downtown in numbers that would rival those of a modern automobile dealer. The 1925 photograph of Brown's Grocery in Vineville (below) shows the greater variety of goods available than in years prior and points the way toward the modern supermarket. (Both, Middle Georgia Archives, Washington Memorial Library.)

The Macon Armory (above) and the original public library (below) stand as excellent examples of the ornate architecture favored in the 19th century even for relatively utilitarian structures. Both of these images date to 1894, and both buildings currently house beautiful event spaces. (Both, Middle Georgia Archives, Washington Memorial Library.)

The Misses Murphy and its employees built one of the most successful women's clothiers in Macon. This photograph is from 1897. (Middle Georgia Archives, Washington Memorial Library.)

The First Baptist Church of Christ building is among the familiar Macon landmarks constructed in the late 19th century. The church's asymmetrical towers distinguish it from the similarly ornate St. Joseph Catholic Church, located next door. (Middle Georgia Archives, Washington Memorial Library.)

In 1871, Mercer University moved to Macon from Penfield. The university has been at the core of the city's intellectual and cultural life for more than 100 years. The administration building (right) was completed in 1874 for $100,000. Below is a 1948 aerial view of the campus. (Right, photograph by Matthew Jennings; below, Middle Georgia Archives, Washington Memorial Library.)

The Procter & Gamble Company, pictured here in 1912, was among Macon's largest employers. (Middle Georgia Archives, Washington Memorial Library.)

In 1887, Tom Woolfolk was accused of murdering nine members of his family—ranging from 18 months to 84 years old—with an axe. During his trial, crowds chanted, "Hang him! Hang him!" In this 1887 photograph, a crowd stands outside the courthouse awaiting the verdict. When Woolfolk did finally hang in 1890, an estimated 10,000 spectators attended. (Middle Georgia Archives, Washington Memorial Library.)

Newspapers were engines that propelled the New South as much as factories. This 1876 image shows the Cherry Street home of the *Macon Telegraph*. The newspaper provided a steady diet of news and optimistic promises from its inception in the 1830s until the present. (Middle Georgia Archives, Washington Memorial Library.)

Four

MAKIN' IT IN MACON
LABOR AND LEISURE
IN THE EARLY 1900S

Maconites worked hard, played hard, and prayed hard in the early 20th century. Cotton and its associated industries remained the most important economic drivers, though the boll weevil's 1917 arrival boded ill for the future. The population grew at an extraordinary rate in the early 20th century, jumping from 23,272 in 1900 to 52,995 in 1920. The automobile arrived in Macon in 1901, and by the 1920s, the town could boast more than 30 miles of paved streets (with more in the surrounding county). Macon grew geographically, too, expanding to include the formerly separate villages of Vineville, East Macon, and South Macon.

Education remained separate and unequal in the early 20th century, but several black-owned businesses thrived, and the Douglass Theatre, owned by Charles Douglass, drew national touring acts to entertain Macon's black community. Some of Macon's most notable public buildings date to this time period, including the City Auditorium, the Washington Memorial Library, the federal courthouse, and the Bibb County Courthouse. In 1912, Confederate veterans flocked to Macon for a reunion, and white Maconites celebrated the legacy of the Confederacy. In 1917, as the United States prepared to enter World War I, thousands of young men from all over Georgia came to train at Fort Wheeler. Macon continued to consider its own history in public ways, too. To celebrate its centennial in 1923, Macon produced a pageant that commemorated important events in the town's past. Religion continued to play a crucial role in the life of the community. Approximately 80 congregations called Macon home by 1920, with Methodists and Baptists representing the largest denominations.

This time period also witnessed the notorious lynching of John "Cocky" Glover, a suspect in a pool hall shooting. In 1922, white Maconites took Glover from police custody, lynched him, and returned his mutilated corpse to Macon, where they dumped the body in the foyer of the Douglass Theatre as part of a larger effort to terrorize Macon's black community.

This photograph, taken during a Civil War veterans' reunion in 1912, overlooks the corner of Third and Cherry Streets. The building under construction in the foreground is the Hotel Dempsey, a downtown Macon landmark. (Middle Georgia Archives, Washington Memorial Library.)

When it opened in 1912, the Hotel Dempsey billed itself as Macon's premier destination for travelers and visiting dignitaries. For many years, its beauty and central location made it just that. In its early years, it even contained a Japanese tea room. (Middle Georgia Archives, Washington Memorial Library.)

In 1923, Macon celebrated its centennial in style by putting on a pageant featuring scenes from the town's past. Here, Alfred Willingham portrays Hernando de Soto, and Mrs. Henry Davis portrays a native woman named Xualla. (Middle Georgia Archives, Washington Memorial Library.)

The citizens of Macon turned out in droves to see William Howard Taft when he came to town in November 1908. A carriage strained to pull the president through a massive arch of cotton bales erected on Second Street for the occasion. In this photograph, Taft addresses a crowd in Central City Park. (Middle Georgia Archives, Washington Memorial Library.)

Charles Douglass was born in 1870 in dire poverty in Macon's Unionville neighborhood. A description of his early life appears in *Macon's Black Heritage: The Untold Story*: "I had to work as soon as I was large enough to earn money. . . . I went out and chopped cotton when I was so small that I had to use a short handle hoe and the pay was only fifteen cents a day." By the early 1900s, Douglass had moved from bicycle repair to real estate. In 1915, Douglass's annual income reached $42,000, and he remained deeply invested in Macon's black community until his death in 1940. (Middle Georgia Archives, Washington Memorial Library.)

Paul Duval was working at Willingham Furniture in the 1880s when he realized he would need to earn more money to educate his children. He started several small businesses before getting into upholstery. In the 1990s, his grandson William (pictured at right with older brother Paul III), wrote that "[my grandfather] looked for every opportunity to make his business successful and it made a difference." Duval and Son is one of Macon's oldest black-owned businesses. (Middle Georgia Archives, Washington Memorial Library.)

DOUGLAS THEATRE
C. H. DOUGLAS, PROPRIETOR

The Douglass Theatre, advertised (and misspelled) on the 1918 card shown above, was Macon's premier black-owned theater from 1911 to 1940. Douglass also owned the adjacent hotel and a café. In the early 20th century, the Douglass Theatre drew national touring acts like Bessie Smith and Gertrude "Ma" Rainey. In 1922, the theater formed the backdrop for a grisly scene as a white lynch mob left the body of John Glover in the lobby to serve as a warning to Macon's black population. (Both, Middle Georgia Archives, Washington Memorial Library.)

Hutchings-Hubbard Undertakers was one of a number of black-owned businesses that flourished in the early 20th century. This photograph captures a 1910 funeral procession as it prepares to move down Forsyth Street. Today, this site is occupied by H&H, a landmark soul food restaurant. (Middle Georgia Archives, Washington Memorial Library.)

Brunner's Drug Store stood at 559 Broadway. This photograph shows the soda fountain as it appeared in 1905. The young man on the right is Julian A. Smith. (Middle Georgia Archives, Washington Memorial Library.)

Dolly Blount Lamar was one of Macon's most prominent citizens in the early 20th century, and she was deeply invested in the memory of the Confederacy, serving as president of the United Daughters of the Confederacy and working to complete a massive memorial on Stone Mountain. In the 1910s, she opposed female suffrage, fearing it would damage state sovereignty and lead to black women voting. This 1917 photograph shows a costume party she hosted that seems to mix Confederate and Colonial imagery. Lamar published a memoir in 1952 titled *When All Is Said and Done*. (Middle Georgia Archives, Washington Memorial Library.)

This trading card, produced around 1910 by the American Tobacco Company, features James Lafitte of the Macon Peaches. The team represented Macon in the South Atlantic League in the early 20th century. (Library of Congress.)

Macon architect Elam Alexander bequeathed the money for the Alexander Free School, also known as Alexander I. The school board eventually used Alexander's gift to found several more schools. Louise M. Napier's sixth-grade class is pictured here in 1909. (Middle Georgia Archives, Washington Memorial Library.)

Several sites around Macon have hosted automobile races over the years. Above, racers in open-top cars whip around the Idle Hour Farm Track in 1915. Below, stock cars kick up dust in Central City Park in an undated photograph. (Both, Middle Georgia Archives, Washington Memorial Library)

The South Lanier High School or Prep Quint

In 1922, the Lanier High School boys' basketball team won the seven-team GIAA tournament and the state championship. The coach that year was Charlie Morgan, and the tournament stretched over three days in February, with games held at the YMCA and the newly opened City Auditorium. In what must have been a barn burner of a championship game, Lanier defeated Tech High by a score of 39 to 38. (Middle Georgia Archives, Washington Memorial Library.)

Lanier High School opened on Forsyth Street in 1913. The seating arrangement here prefigures the separation of boys and girls into separate schools starting in 1924. The girls remained in the Forsyth Street building until 1932, when the A.L. Miller Senior High School for Girls opened on Montpelier Avenue. (Middle Georgia Archives, Washington Memorial Library.)

SENIOR CLASS LANIER HIGH SCHOOL 1915

Macon's Camp Wheeler, pictured below, was a central site used for the training of the soldiers who would join the American Expeditionary Force in World War I. Soldiers from Camp Wheeler found themselves in France by February 1918 as members of the 151st Machine Gun Battalion. Before their deployment, the white soldiers were honored with a parade down Cherry Street. Black soldiers from Macon trained at a separate fort in Atlanta and were primarily employed in menial labor. (Both, Middle Georgia Archives, Washington Memorial Library.)

Macon's downtown skyline was transformed in the early 20th century, and many of the most significant public buildings date to that era. The City Auditorium was intended to replace a huge wooden structure thrown together in 1917 for a music and arts festival called the Chautauqua of the South. The 6,500-seat City Auditorium opened in 1925; it was constructed from limestone and topped with a copper dome reputed to be the largest in the world. In this c. 1930 photograph, the auditorium is flanked by Stroberg's body shop, a barber, and the YMCA. The YMCA later closed its doors rather than accept African American members. Today, the Macon Health Club occupies the old YMCA building. (Middle Georgia Archives, Washington Memorial Library.)

The Commercial National Bank stood on the triangular block where Cotton Avenue and Second Street split. After the Confederate Memorial was placed in the small park adjacent to the bank, it was renamed the Confederate Building. (Middle Georgia Archives, Washington Memorial Library.)

Gate to Central City Park, Home of Georgia State Fair, Macon, Ga.

In his 1879 *Historical Record of Macon and Central Georgia*, John C. Butler notes that Central City Park "embraces two hundred and fifty acres of level land, the whole delightfully shaded by a native growth of monster oaks, and ornamented with flowers." The city funded a massive program of improvements at the park in 1871 for $300,000. By the early 20th century, it included a track, playing fields, and various buildings associated with the state fair, which is held in Macon every year. The round building, pictured below in 1961, is currently slated for a major renovation. (Above, Matthew Jennings; below, Middle Georgia Archives, Washington Memorial Library.)

71

In this c. 1910 image, employees of the Daniel & Blasingame Company pose in front of the shop at 655 Poplar Street (now 665 Poplar Street). In the early 20th century, African Americans often found low-paying employment as messengers and delivery men in Macon. (Middle Georgia Archives, Washington Memorial Library.)

Horses and wagons still traversed the intersection of Cotton Avenue and Mulberry Street as late as the 1910s. Today, the building on the corner houses a florist, and shops on Cotton Avenue include a bakery, a music store, a bookstore, and the offices of the Otis Redding Foundation. (Middle Georgia Archives, Washington Memorial Library.)

POST OFFICE BUILDING AT MACON, GA.

This building, completed in 1908, currently houses a federal courthouse and a post office. It replaced a brick federal building that had stood on the site since 1889. Today, it is named for Judge William Augustus Bootle, who presided over several key cases dealing with integration in transportation and education. The statue honors William Wadley, president of the Central of Georgia Railway when the railroad rebuilt after the Civil War. (Matthew Jennings.)

Macon began hosting the Georgia State Fair in 1871 and has continued to do so with only a few interruptions. This photograph was taken at the midway in 1927. (Middle Georgia Archives, Washington Memorial Library.)

Happp Brothers' Clothing Company, located at Pine Street and Broadway, was a major supplier of military gear during World War II and one of Macon's largest employers in the middle of the 20th century. (Middle Georgia Archives, Washington Memorial Library.)

This horse, the carriage, and these young women—Martha Johnson and Edith Dean Stetson—are decked out in finery for a spring parade in 1900. The photograph was taken at the corner of First and Mulberry Streets. (Middle Georgia Archives, Washington Memorial Library.)

Theodore "Tiger" Flowers, born in
Camilla in 1895, fought throughout
Georgia, including in Macon, Brunswick,
and Atlanta, and around the country.
In 1926, he won the middleweight
championship, becoming the first African
American to achieve that distinction. In
addition to his athletic prowess, Flowers
was known for his piety. He carried a Bible
into the ring and earned the nickname
"Georgia Deacon" as a result. He died in
1927 after an operation and was grieved
throughout Georgia. (Middle Georgia
Archives, Washington Memorial Library.)

Tiger Flowers

Boxer W.L. "Young" Stribling's
Vaudevillian family settled in Macon
in the 1910s. Stribling notched his
first professional fight as a teenager
and went on to an illustrious, if ill-
fated, career. He came frustratingly
close to being crowned heavyweight
champion of the world, losing to Max
Schmeling in the 15th round in 1931.
Stribling died in a motorcycle accident
in 1933. (Middle Georgia Archives,
Washington Memorial Library.)

This horse race took place at Central City Park in 1913. (Middle Georgia Archives, Washington Memorial Library.)

Well-dressed women and men toss horseshoes in this 1915 photograph. (Middle Georgia Archives, Washington Memorial Library.)

It is likely that Cleopatra Love's mother, Laura, a renowned dressmaker, sewed this dress for her daughter (pictured as a teenager in 1910) upon her graduation from the Green Street School. Cleopatra Love had a long teaching career in Atlanta and Florida but retired to Macon, where she passed away in 1982. (Middle Georgia Archives, Washington Memorial Library.)

Sen. Augustus O. Bacon donated 100 acres of land on the Ocmulgee's east side for the Masonic Home. Originally, the home, which opened in 1905, cared for both the elderly and children, but over time, its mission evolved to focus on residential care for children in need. (Matthew Jennings.)

MASONIC HOME OF GEORGIA, MACON, GA.—5

Low wages for industrial jobs made child labor a fact of life in many parts of the United States in the early 20th century, and Macon was no exception. Reformer Lewis Hine hoped to change that by documenting the harsh conditions under which children labored. He visited Macon in 1909 and took pictures at several mills, including Bibb Mill No. 1, where he captured both of these images. (Both, Library of Congress.)

This type of wordplay—exchanging "Macon" for "makin' "—has proven irresistible for a very long time, as demonstrated by this 1917 Loos Brothers, Jack Frost, and Paul Biese composition. (Matthew Jennings.)

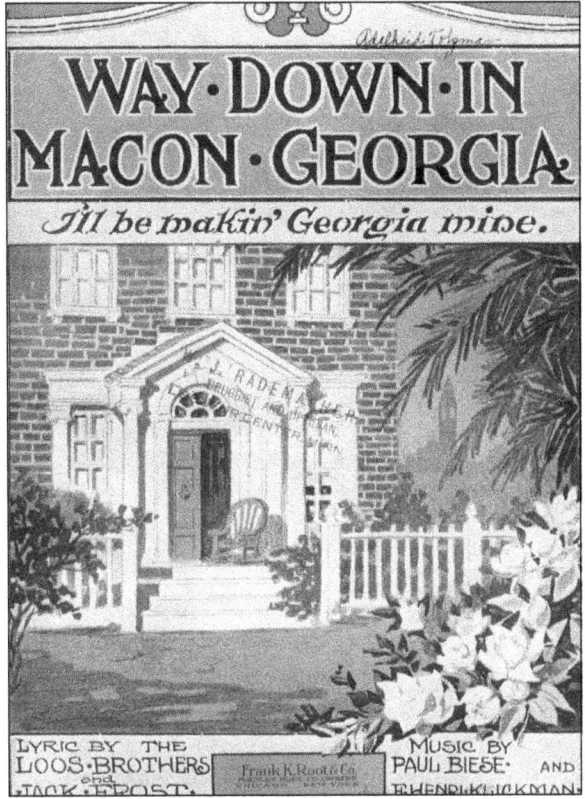

This striking image, taken during the Confederate veterans' reunion in 1912, shows the third Bibb County Courthouse, near the right side of the image, which stood from 1870 until 1924. (Middle Georgia Archives, Washington Memorial Library.)

Mulberry St from [illegible] St Looking South Showi[ng]

This image, taken from atop the 1870 Bibb County Courthouse, looks down Mulberry Street. The 1857 Washington Block remains one of downtown's more alluring buildings. (Middle Georgia Archives, Washington Memorial Library.)

The fourth and current Bibb County Courthouse, pictured here in the 1940s, was completed in 1924 in a Neoclassical Revival style. (Middle Georgia Archives, Washington Memorial Library.)

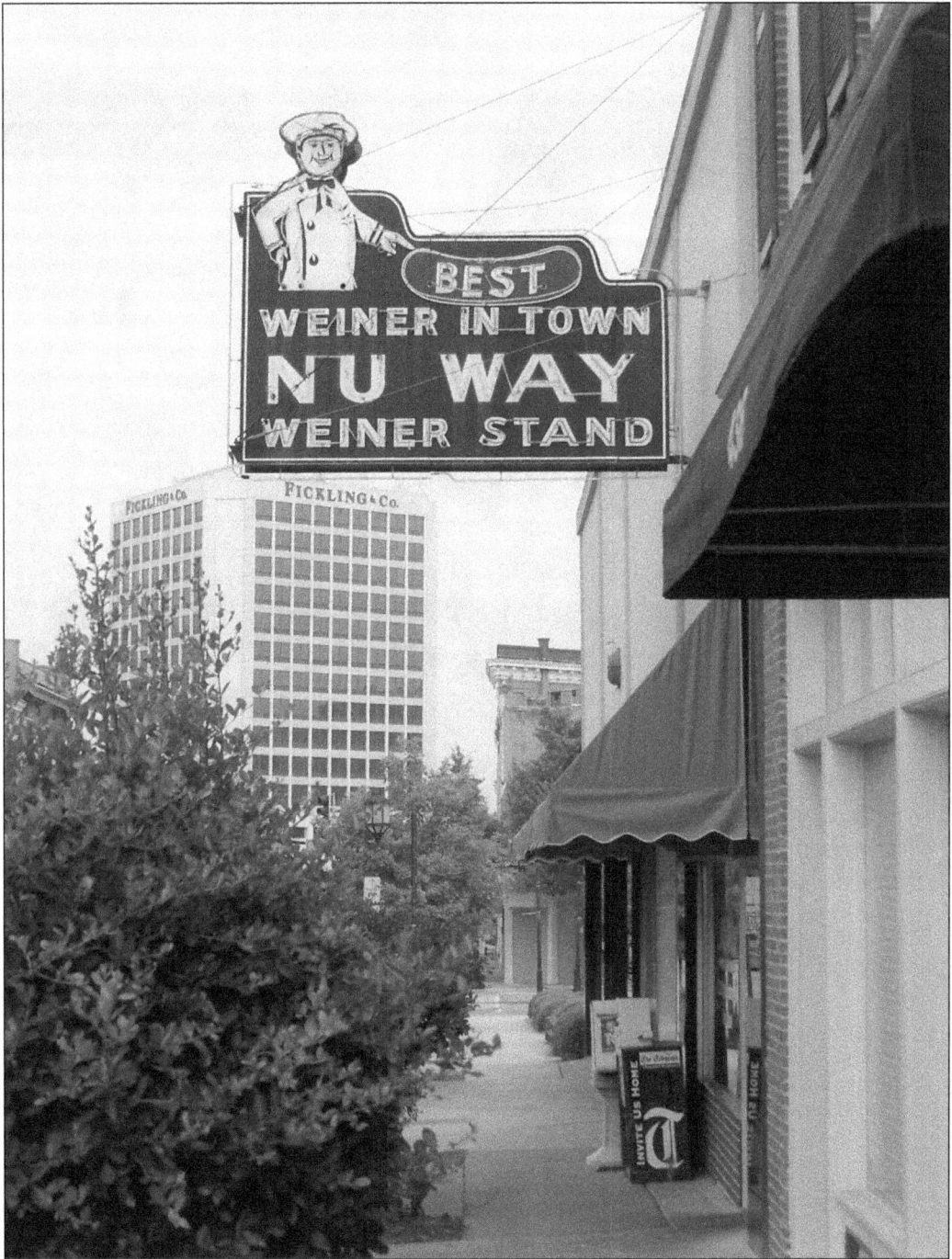

Few foods are as quintessentially Macon as a Nu-Way weiner. The Cotton Avenue fixture has been serving bright-red hot dogs "all the way"—with chili, mustard, and onions—since the 1910s. (Photograph by Matthew Jennings.)

The offices of Procter & Gamble were located in the 400 and 500 blocks of Poplar Street. This 1926 photograph shows workers leaving with Christmas gift baskets. (Middle Georgia Archives, Washington Memorial Library.)

Macon residents attended baseball games at Luther Williams Field, which is pictured here around 1955. (Middle Georgia Archives, Washington Memorial Library.)

In the mid-1920s, Wesleyan College's College Street campus was deemed insufficient for the growing school's needs. By 1928, the college had moved to this location on Forsythe Road. The Candler Building, today's alumnae center, originally served as the new campus's library. (Photograph by Matthew Jennings.)

The 1911 Georgia State Fair was a scene of tragedy when pioneering aviator Eugene Ely crashed in Central City Park. The pilot jumped clear of the wreck but broke his neck on impact and died almost immediately. Ely was only 25 years old. (Middle Georgia Archives, Washington Memorial Library.)

Five

ROCK, SOUL, AND RIGHTS
THE SOUNDS OF DISCONTENT

Macon grew by leaps and bounds in the years immediately after World War II. Money and people flowed into the region as a result of the military mobilization of the 1940s, and Macon benefited.

As agricultural production in Georgia shifted from smaller, family-owned farms worked by tenants to larger, more industrial operations, rural Georgians, many of them African American, moved to Macon. Wealthier white Maconites reflected larger national trends when they moved to suburban areas. Census data shows dramatic growth in Macon's population, which reached 125,000 by 1970, reflecting expansion in the older parts of town as well as the annexation of surrounding suburban areas.

As Macon's black population surged, calls for full equality before the law grew louder. While some white Maconites supported the aims of the civil rights movement, many more were recalcitrant, and some even took up arms to terrorize African Americans. African Americans boycotted, participated in sit-ins, and began to flex their collective political muscle. While white Macon was never as vicious and violent as the resistance to integration that rocked other Southern cities, it fought against black equality, and all of Macon suffered as a result. Race remains one of the most persistent dividing lines in Macon.

Very few towns of Macon's size can lay claim to such a rich musical heritage. From the supercharged early rock 'n' roll of Little Richard to the sweet soul of Otis Redding to the driving Southern rock of the Allman Brothers Band, Macon means music, and American music would not be the same without Macon's outsized influence.

Neva Jane Langley, a Florida-born woman studying at Wesleyan College, relaxes backstage at the 1952 Miss Macon Pageant. Langley went on to win the Miss America pageant in 1953. (Middle Georgia Archives, Washington Memorial Library.)

When it opened in 1949, Ballard-Hudson High School was the only public school that taught African Americans past the eighth grade. At left, Ruth Hartley Mosley helps members of the Delta Tri-Hi-Y Club prepare for the annual Easter lily sale in 1954. (Middle Georgia Archives, Washington Memorial Library.)

In 1950, the Macon Peaches, a Class A team, finished with a record of 90 wins against 63 losses and won the South Atlantic League. (Middle Georgia Archives, Washington Memorial Library.)

The Milwaukee Braves visited Macon's Luther Williams Field in 1954. Henry "Hank" Aaron is at left, and Andy Pafko is at right. (Middle Georgia Archives, Washington Memorial Library.)

The women's clubhouse at Baconsfield, pictured in 1958, served as a gathering place for various social organizations. (Middle Georgia Archives, Washington Memorial Library.)

Baconsfield Park included walking paths, lagoons, playing fields, and even a petting zoo, as shown in this 1955 image. (Middle Georgia Archives, Washington Memorial Library.)

Augustus Bacon, a US senator from Macon, deeded over 100 acres of land on the east side of the Ocmulgee for a park for the exclusive use of "white women, white girls, white boys and white children." In 1963, black attempts to integrate the park were threatened by a caretaker waving a pistol at them. Eventually, once the Supreme Court ruled that such public discrimination was unconstitutional, the park reverted to the ownership of Bacon's heirs, who sold the property to developers in the early 1970s rather than open the park to all citizens of Macon. In the words of historian Andrew Manis, Macon's white population "sacrificed the general welfare of the city and the park to the gods of greed and Jim Crow." Today, the land that once contained the park houses a shopping center and an apartment complex. (Above, Matthew Jennings; below, Middle Georgia Archives, Washington Memorial Library.)

Striking inequality between Macon's black and white populations combined with black activism, on the part of Willis Sheftall Sr. and others, to convince the Works Progress Administration to choose Macon as one of the sites for a new style of community center, the Booker T. Washington Community Center (BTWCC), in 1938. Sheftall was named director of the center and served in that post for more than 50 years. (Middle Georgia Archives, Washington Memorial Library.)

Through its history, the BTWCC has offered many different enrichment activities. This unidentified class is pictured in the 1940s. (Middle Georgia Archives, Washington Memorial Library.)

In this 1958 photograph from the Booker T. Washington Community Center, beginner sewing students work on the hemline of a young woman's dress. (Middle Georgia Archives, Washington Memorial Library.).

This 1964 photograph shows members of a band class at the Booker T. Washington Community Center. (Middle Georgia Archives, Washington Memorial Library.)

This 1970 display at the Booker T. Washington Community Center highlights the historic achievements of African Americans. (Middle Georgia Archives, Washington Memorial Library.)

The Booker T. Washington Community Center was not all work all the time. Here, members of the homemakers' club throw a New Year's Eve party to welcome the arrival of 1954. (Middle Georgia Archives, Washington Memorial Library.)

James Brown was born in South Carolina, raised in Augusta, and first hit it big with the help of Macon promoter Clint Brantley. Brantley commissioned this and other publicity shots for Brown, the leader of the Famous Flames, in 1957. (Middle Georgia Archives, Washington Memorial Library.)

Street singer Rev. Pearly Brown was a fixture in downtown Macon for decades. He achieved his greatest recorded successes in the 1960s and 1970s, including classic folk blues albums such as *Georgia Street Singer* and *It's a Mean Old World to Try to Live In*, but those who heard him live and on record swear by the energy of the live performances, which Brown often interspersed with preaching. (Middle Georgia Archives, Washington Memorial Library.)

The 500 block of Cotton Avenue was one of several sections of downtown Macon where black businesses flourished. Dr. D.T. Walton bought the triangular building on the corner in 1936 to use as a dentist's office. His son practiced in the same building. (Middle Georgia Archives, Washington Memorial Library.)

As part of the ceremonies surrounding the dedication of the Ocmulgee National Monument visitor center in 1951, a Muscogee (Creek) delegation visited Macon. Inclement weather forced the stickball demonstration into the City Auditorium. (Ocmulgee National Monument, National Park Service.)

The Douglass Theatre snack bar, pictured here in 1956, served the downtown black community. (Middle Georgia Archives, Washington Memorial Library.)

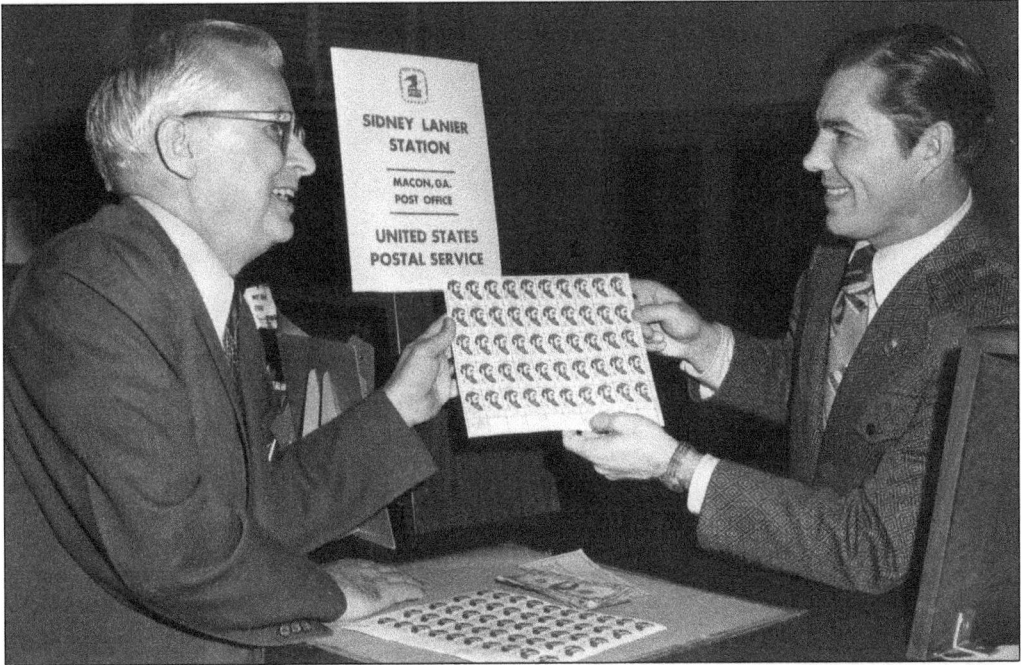

Ronnie Thompson, sometimes called "Machine Gun Ronnie" for his rough handling of racial tension, was mayor of Macon from 1967 to 1975. In this 1972 photograph, Thompson (right) purchases commemorative Sidney Lanier stamps from an unidentified postal employee. (Middle Georgia Archives, Washington Memorial Library.)

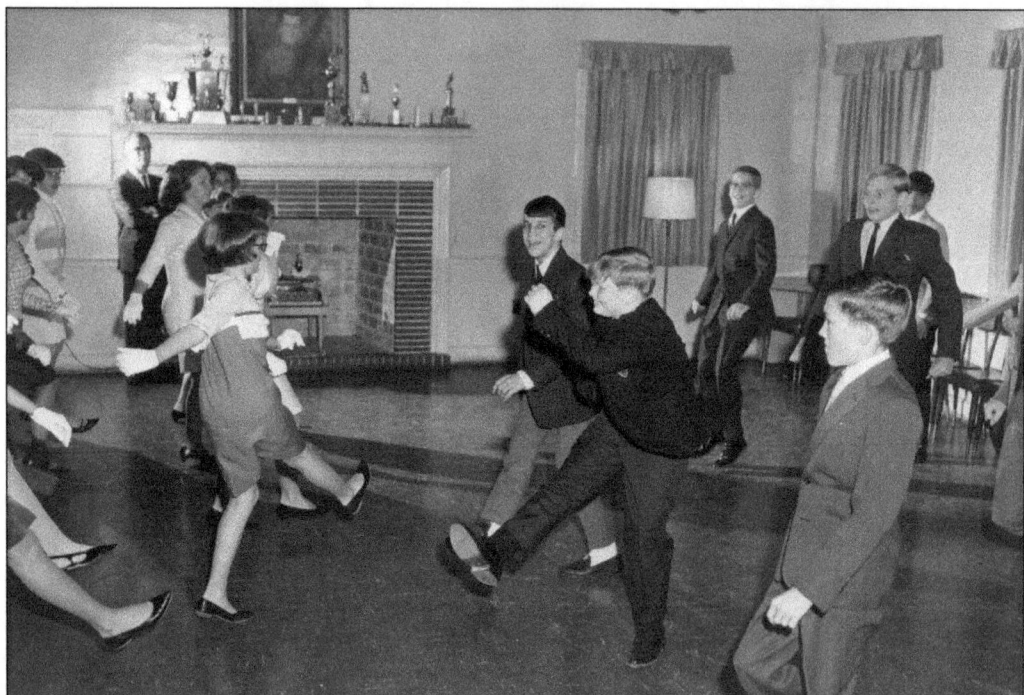

American Legion Post No. 3 hosted this spirited teen dance party in February 1966. (Middle Georgia Archives, Washington Memorial Library.)

The Georgia Academy for the Blind was established in Macon in 1856 and moved to its current home on Vineville Avenue in 1902. Blind students of color attended the Negro Division of the Academy for the Blind. In this early-20th-century picture, students study in the library. (Middle Georgia Archives, Washington Memorial Library.)

Pleasant Hill, established in 1879, was initially inhabited in large part by former slaves. The neighborhood was—and remains—a center of Macon's black community life. Minnie Smith founded Beda-Etta College here in 1921 to serve African Americans excluded by the discriminatory school system. Other key sites include Linwood Cemetery, Mattie Hubbard Jones Park, and a number of historic churches. There are currently fewer businesses and schools in Pleasant Hill than in years past. Many of Pleasant Hill's troubles can be traced to the 1960s construction of Interstate 75 through the heart of the neighborhood. (Above, Middle Georgia Archives, Washington Memorial Library; below, photograph by Matthew Jennings.)

Alvin Luke Gonder (also known as Fats Gonder and Count Basic) was a key figure in the Macon music scene of the mid-20th century. In the words of Preston Lauterbach, author of *The Chitlin' Circuit and the Road to Rock 'n' Roll*, Gonder "taught Little Richard beginning piano chops, helped discover James Brown and the Famous Flames, and nicknamed Brown 'the hardest working man in show business.'" (Middle Georgia Archives, Washington Memorial Library.)

On March 23, 1968—just weeks before he was assassinated—Dr. Martin Luther King Jr. visited Macon and spoke at New Zion Baptist Church. (Middle Georgia Archives, Washington Memorial Library.)

Richard Penniman—"Little Richard"—was raised in Macon's Pleasant Hill and began to hit the big time in 1954 with his flamboyant stage presence, hard-rocking piano riffs, and unique vocal style. He honed his skills performing in drag and minstrel shows and exploded on the rock 'n' roll scene with such force that he earned the sobriquet "Quasar of Rock 'n' Roll." In 1955, he recorded a cleaned-up version of his fierce club hit "Tutti Frutti," which reached no. 17 on the pop chart and no. 2 on the R&B chart in 1956. In the 1954 image above, Little Richard, resplendent in his cape and pompadour, performs at Ann's Tic Toc Room on Broadway. At right is a promotional photograph that he distributed when he played shows in his hometown in the 1970s. (Both, Middle Georgia Archives, Washington Memorial Library.)

Building on traditions of activism and drawing strength from politically engaged churches, Macon's African American community took to the streets to protest injustice in the 1960s and 1970s. In the late 1960s, black Maconites were part of a larger protest campaign, the Poor People's Campaign, designed to draw attention to the grinding poverty that was a constant part of too many people's lives. These photographs are from Broadway (above) and Cherry Street (below). (Both, Middle Georgia Archives, Washington Memorial Library.)

July 1971 was a crucial moment in Macon's civil rights history. Mayor Ronnie Thompson had just issued a "shoot-to-kill" order for anyone found violating a curfew. Rev. Julius Caesar Hope (center) led this protest march through downtown accompanied by Marshall Stinson and Harry Randall. Reverend Hope later made headlines when he ran a credible, though unsuccessful, campaign for mayor against Buckner F. Melton. (Both, Middle Georgia Archives, Washington Memorial Library.)

Many of Macon's white residents were willing to go to great lengths to derail meaningful integration and racial equality, although violence, generally speaking, was rare in Macon. Here, a symbol of massive resistance, Lester Maddox, rides his bicycle backwards past the Dixie Sewing Center in March 1969. (Middle Georgia Archives, Washington Memorial Library.)

This civil rights march took place on Cherry Street in May 1968. (Middle Georgia Archives, Washington Memorial Library.)

Ruth Hartley Mosley, pictured here in 1949 at her home on Spring Street with her husband, Fisher, was one of Macon's most prominent African American citizens. She was active in the NAACP, served as a founding board member of the Booker T. Washington Community Center, and was active in the Steward Chapel AME Church. (Middle Georgia Archives, Washington Memorial Library.)

The Ocmulgee National Monument visitor center opened to great fanfare in 1951. At the time, it housed an astounding collection of artifacts from throughout the Southeastern United States, as well as displays celebrating ancient and more recent Native American history. A Creek delegation traveled from Oklahoma for the dedication ceremonies. (Middle Georgia Archives, Washington Memorial Library.)

In 1963, a new post office and federal building was erected on College Street. Designed to echo the first building on the site (Wesleyan College), the building was eventually named for Henry McNeal Turner. Turner was active in the civil rights struggles of the 19th century and was a leading voice for Georgia's African Americans. (Matthew Jennings.)

William P. Randall, also known as "Daddy Bill," was a leader in Macon's black community for decades. He was one of black Macon's pioneers in the early chapters of the movement, fighting for bus desegregation and increased opportunities for African Americans. (Middle Georgia Archives, Washington Memorial Library.)

One of the brightest soul stars of the 1960s, Macon's Otis Redding scored his first hit in 1963 with "These Arms of Mine." He went on to make scores of influential records, balancing poignant ballads with driving horn lines and electric guitar riffs provided by Steve Cropper. Redding's career was cut tragically short when a plane carrying the singer crashed in Madison, Wisconsin, in 1967. After his death, "Sittin' on the Dock of the Bay" sold more than one million copies and hit number one on the pop chart. In image below, Redding is receiving the keys to a new car from his manager, Alan Walden. (Both, Middle Georgia Archives, Washington Memorial Library.)

St. Peter Claver Catholic Church, located at 133 Ward Street, began in 1888 as a parish specifically geared to serve Macon's black community. The building (above) was completed in 1928. St. Peter Claver has functioned, and continues to function, as a vibrant focal point of black life in Macon. (Both, Middle Georgia Archives, Washington Memorial Library.)

The Georgia State Fair has a fascinating—if divided—history when it comes to race. In the early 20th century, an organization called the Georgia Colored Agricultural and Industrial Association put on a Colored Fair in Macon. One year, the Colored Fair even featured a reunion for ex-slaves. When key organizers left the area, the Colored Fair was discontinued. By the middle of the 20th century, blacks and whites could both compete at the Georgia State Fair, though usually in different divisions. (Both, Middle Georgia Archives, Washington Memorial Library.)

In 1959, church members gathered outside of Steward AME Church. (Middle Georgia Archives, Washington Memorial Library.)

Even after de jure segregation crumbled in the 1960s, the words "Colored Waiting Room" remain engraved in the stone of Terminal Station. Their preservation serves as a rare, stark, and tangible reminder of Macon's troubled past. Terminal Station, located at the foot of Cherry Street, was constructed in 1916. Service was strictly segregated until the 1960s, though many railroad employees were African American. Once passenger rail service ceased, Terminal Station fell into disrepair. NewTown Macon recently renovated the building for $5 million before handing it over to the Macon Transit Authority, which made it a regional transportation center. Aficionados continue to hope for a return to passenger rail service, but in the meantime, Terminal Station serves as the Macon Transit Authority's headquarters and is available for event rentals. (Photograph by Matthew Jennings.)

Six

CITY OF CHURCHES, CITY OF CHANGES
MODERN MACON

Religious leaders have often used their authority to justify the status quo or to justify change. They have defended slavery and fought to end it. They have justified segregation and organized against it. They have defined themselves through unity and through separation. Perhaps no force—not even the idea of democracy itself—is as deeply rooted into the Southern psyche as the force of religious authority. Perhaps because of this authority, it is customary—especially in Southern communities—to think of churches as symbols of permanence and stability. But there is more than meets the eye. Congregations have outgrown older facilities and moved on to new ones either nearby or in the suburbs. Old buildings have been put to new uses. Symbols and spaces have been redefined as the community changes. Thus, this book ends where it began, with what anthropologists call "ritual spaces." Such spaces not only include houses of worship—though Macon has touted itself as a "city of churches" for many years—but also buildings and open spaces with physical arrangements highly symbolic of power, authority, ideas, or relationships.

There are some Christian denominations that have called Central Georgia home for more than two centuries, often occupying the same tract of land for the whole time—but with the passage of time, those congregations have welcomed new friends such as Jews, Hindus, and Muslims. The community's devotion to the divine testifies to the cultures that have shaped it. Anthropologists say that religious practices help people define themselves as individuals, as families, and as communities—a process called "identity performance." But religious communities not only help people understand who they are, they also identify people to others. Houses of worship are the physical manifestations of the ideas that have shaped Macon from its beginnings.

At the same time, Macon has built ritual spaces of a different sort—schools, shopping centers, performance venues, monuments, and parks that also tell the stories of the people who have lived and worked there. These, too, are testaments to the values and priorities of the community that built them.

This unusual dedication appears on the archway that serves as the entrance to a cemetery adjacent to the Jesus Mission of Love Holiness Church on Pio Nono Avenue. (Photograph by Matthew Jennings.)

Rev. T.W. Callaway and 28 congregants founded Tabernacle Baptist Church in 1900 in a tent in downtown Macon. The church consistently grew in both population and building size, with the final construction project, an activities building, launched in 1977. The congregation maintained a home at the corner of Second and Arch Streets downtown until 2002, when the church relocated to the rapidly growing Zebulon Road area in northwest Macon. The church also owns a lake several miles away in Musella. (Middle Georgia Archives, Washington Memorial Library.)

Tattnall Square Presbyterian Church, located on College Street, closed in 2011. Flint River Presbytery, which owned the building, donated it to Mercer University. The university announced in 2013 that it plans to turn the building into the Tattnall Square Center for the Arts. (Photograph by Stephen Wallace Taylor.)

One of Macon's oldest downtown congregations, St. Joseph Catholic Church, dates from 1841. Construction of the current building began in 1889 and was completed 14 years later. With its twin spires reaching 200 feet into the air and more than 60 stained glass windows (many imported from Germany), the church building is among Macon's most recognizable landmarks. (Middle Georgia Archives, Washington Memorial Library.)

First Baptist Church of Christ, founded in 1826, has occupied this distinctive building since 1887. Its ornate architecture is similar to that of the St. Joseph Catholic Church, which was constructed across the street a few years later. In the early 1990s, First Baptist joined the new Cooperative Baptist Fellowship, a group advocating a more progressive approach than the increasingly conservative Southern Baptist Convention. (Middle Georgia Archives, Washington Memorial Library.)

Ten believers under the leadership of Rev. R.B. Williams launched the Macedonia Missionary Baptist Church in 1893. In 1999, the African American congregation, now simply known as Macedonia Church, had outgrown its Hazel Street home and acquired this property on Eisenhower Parkway when Mabel White Baptist Church relocated to suburban Bass Road. The church has had only six permanent pastors in its 120-year history, a testament to the significance of forceful personal leadership in the congregation. (Photograph by Stephen Wallace Taylor.)

In 1999, Mabel White Baptist Church moved to new quarters along Bass Road in north Macon. Most of the members already lived in the northern suburban neighborhoods, and the new location offered room for growth. (Photograph by Stephen Wallace Taylor.)

German Orthodox Jews established Temple Beth Israel, Macon's oldest Jewish congregation, in 1859, but by 1880, the group had joined the Reform Judaism movement. The group's first permanent home on Poplar Street proved too noisy on Saturdays due to its proximity to the City Market. The current building, at the corner of Spring and Cherry Streets, was completed in 1902. While this building was under construction, the congregation worshipped at the nearby First Baptist Church. (Photograph by Matthew Jennings.)

A later generation of emigrants from eastern Europe, with more conservative ideas than those in circulation at Beth Israel, formed Congregation Sha'arey Israel in 1904. This group met in rented halls until the current structure was completed in 1922. (Photograph by Stephen Wallace Taylor.)

High Street Unitarian Universalist Church was chartered in 1979 and held its first regular meetings in the basement of a downtown bank building. Today, the congregation meets in this building on High Street, which was originally built for the First Christian Church (Disciples of Christ) in 1898 and later housed the Central Church of Christ. (Photograph by Stephen Wallace Taylor.)

The United House of Prayer for All People sits on Emery Highway across from Coliseum Medical Center. The building's distinctive multicolored brickwork and elaborate flanking sculptures mark it as unique, while the concept of a religious organization that is truly "for all people" suggests a lofty aspiration for the future of the city and for people everywhere. (Photograph by Stephen Wallace Taylor.)

Religious structures often change not just ownership but also affiliation, sometimes rather dramatically. This structure on Vineville Avenue, former home of a Primitive Baptist church, has housed the Islamic Center of Macon since 2009. (Photograph by Stephen Wallace Taylor.)

In 2003, immigrants from the Indian state of Gujarat established Shree Umiya Mataji Mandir, a Hindu temple, on Raley Road in southwest Macon. (Photograph by Stephen Wallace Taylor.)

The Big House Museum, located at 2321 Vineville Avenue in a house formerly inhabited by several members of the Allman Brothers Band, preserves the heritage of the band as well as presenting live music in an outdoor concert venue. (Photograph by Matthew Jennings.)

The Broadway Lofts, one of a spate of recent rehabilitation projects, occupy the building formerly owned by the Happ Brothers Company. (Photograph by Matthew Jennings.)

The Capitol Theatre, located on Second Street, first opened for business in 1916. The building suffered 30 years of neglect after it shut down in 1976, but the early 21st century has brought a remarkable turnaround. The Cox Capitol Theatre, which reopened in 2006, regularly hosts national acts, local favorites, and movies for families and grown-ups alike. (Photograph by Matthew Jennings.)

The Georgia State Board of Education and the Bibb County Board of Education created the Macon Area Vocational-Technical School in 1962. The school initially had three locations. In the mid-1970s, high demand for the school's services spurred the construction of a new facility off of Eisenhower Parkway on Macon Tech Drive. In 2000, the school assumed its current name, and Central Georgia Technical College, offering nearly 200 programs of study, remains a key player in training skilled workers. (Photograph by Matthew Jennings.)

Today, Central City Park remains one of Macon's most popular gathering places. The wide grassy areas and groves of trees serve as the settings for scores of family reunions, cookouts, and birthday parties. The locomotive pictured at right, a 2-8-0 "Consolidation" engine, was built in 1906 and decommissioned in 1959. It stands in Central City Park as a monument to Benny Scott, the first black fireman on the Central of Georgia Railway. (Photographs by Matthew Jennings.)

Local realtor William Fickling Sr. was obsessed with a pink blooming tree he found in his backyard in the 1940s. Upon discovering that it was a Yoshino cherry tree, Fickling shared his love—and many of the trees—with Macon. Today, there may be as many as 300,000 Yoshino cherry trees throughout Macon, and when they are in bloom, the effect is nothing short of breathtaking. The Cherry Blossom Festival began in 1982 and has expanded to become a 10-day celebration of "love, beauty, and international friendship" and grown to become a significant tourist draw in the region. (Photograph by David Jennings.)

The Macon Coliseum was built in 1968. It was a state-of-the-art entertainment facility at the time, and a series of renovations have allowed it to continue to offer high-quality acts from around the country. The roof reportedly echoes the shape of the Great Temple Mound at Ocmulgee. (Photograph by Matthew Jennings.)

Recent years have seen a resurgence in the desirability of downtown real estate, and one of the results has been increased attention to unused industrial space. As of this writing, occupancy in the downtown area is hovering around 90 percent. New loft projects are kicking into gear on Cherry Street (at right) and in the former Dannenberg Building, a Third Street department store with roots in the 19th century. Another feature of the revitalized downtown is the Ocmulgee Heritage Trail, also known as the River Walk. NewTown Macon and the Department of Parks and Recreation partner to care for the 11-mile-long trail and its nearly 1,500 acres of associated green spaces. When the weather is nice, one can expect to see many people enjoying this important resource. (Photographs by Matthew Jennings.)

The Hotel Dempsey had fallen into decline when it was reborn in 1981 with a mission to provide subsidized apartments for elderly residents and people with disabilities. The ground floor now houses a number of businesses, including a popular Mexican restaurant. (Photograph by Matthew Jennings.)

The Douglass Theatre, once the premier entertainment center for Macon's black community, shut its doors—seemingly for good—in the 1970s. In the 1990s, dedicated Maconites lovingly restored the landmark, and it now hosts a diverse array of films, cultural events, and live musical performances. (Photograph by Matthew Jennings.)

The Allman Brothers Band formed in Jacksonville, Florida, in 1969, but a contract with Capricorn Records brought the group to Macon shortly thereafter. The band's first lineup included Duane Allman on lead and slide guitar, Greg Allman (Duane's brother) on organ and vocals, Dickey Betts on guitar, Raymond "Berry" Oakley on bass, and Jai Johanny "Jaimoe" Johanson and Butch Trucks on drums. The band reached the mountaintop with their 1971 album *At Fillmore East* and established themselves as leading practitioners of blues-derived Southern rock. On the heels of this massive commercial success, Duane Allman perished in a motorcycle accident in Macon in October 1971. Just as the band began to recover, Oakley met the same fate a little over a year later and a few blocks away. Allman and Oakley are buried next to each other in Rose Hill Cemetery. The Allman Brothers Band has gone through many incarnations in the years since and put out some fine albums but has yet to discover a combination that recaptures the magic of the late 1960s and early 1970s. (Above, Middle Georgia Archives, Washington Memorial Library; below, photograph by Matthew Jennings.)

This building at 430 Cherry Street dates to 1888 and housed the *Evening News,* a now-defunct newspaper. The space was reborn in 2005 as the Hummingbird Stage and Taproom. The Hummingbird books a mix of nationally known acts and regional up-and-comers. (Photograph by Matthew Jennings.)

The Ocmulgee Indian Celebration began in 1991 as an effort to increase awareness of Macon's Native American heritage, deepen the connection between removed Southeastern nations and Ocmulgee, and attract and educate tourists from throughout the Southeast. The celebration is still going strong two decades later and draws nearly 20,000 visitors for the two-day event. This photograph is from the 1990s. (National Park Service, Ocmulgee National Monument.)

Macon State College began in 1968 as Macon Junior College with just over 1,000 students. By the early 21st century, enrollment had soared to more than 6,000 students, and the college offered bachelor's degrees in a variety of fields. In 2013, Macon State and Middle Georgia College combined to form Middle Georgia State College. (Middle Georgia State College.)

The Georgia Sports Hall of Fame traces its origins to 1956. That year, the Georgia Athletic Coaches Association founded a Prep Sports Hall of Fame. From these humble beginnings, the Georgia Sports Hall of Fame, located at 301 Cherry Street in Macon, has grown to become the largest state sports hall of fame in the United States. The hall opened at its current site in 1999. (Photograph by Matthew Jennings.)

In 1967, Marine sergeant Rodney Davis threw himself on a live grenade in Vietnam in an effort to save the lives of his comrades. He was posthumously awarded the Medal of Honor for this brave and selfless act. In November 2012, after a brief fundraising campaign led by the 1/5 Vietnam Veterans Association, a new monument to Davis was installed in Linwood Cemetery. (Photograph by Matthew Jennings.)

The Tubman African American Museum was the brainchild of Fr. Richard Keil, who was assigned to St. Peter Claver Catholic Church in 1976. Father Keil deeply identified with the struggles of his parishioners and sought to create an institution that would celebrate African American history and culture. In 1985, the museum came to life in a formerly abandoned building at 340 Walnut Street. By the early 21st century, the museum welcomed 65,000 visitors annually. Currently, plans are in effect to move the museum to a new setting on Cherry Street near Terminal Station and the Georgia Sports Hall of Fame. (Photograph by Matthew Jennings.)

BIBLIOGRAPHY

Anderson, Nancy Briska. *Macon: A Pictorial History*. Virginia Beach: Donning Company for the Middle Georgia Historical Society, 1979.

Barfield, James. *Historic Macon: An Illustrated History*. San Antonio: Historical Publishing Network for the Historic Macon Foundation, 2007.

Bellamy, Donnie D. "Macon, Georgia, 1823-1860: A Study in Urban Slavery." *Phylon* 45 (1984): 298–310.

Bozeman, Glenda Barnes. *Macon*. Charleston, SC: Arcadia Publishing, 2010.

Butler, John C. *Historical Record of Macon and Central Georgia*. Macon: Middle Georgia Historical Society, 1969. Orig. 1879.

Darnell, Conie Mac. *Walking on Cotton: Civil War and Emancipation Era Guide to Macon, GA*. Tallahassee: Rose Digital, 2011.

Hally, David J., ed. *Ocmulgee Archaeology, 1936–1986*. Athens: University of Georgia Press, 1994.

Herring, Jeanne. *Macon, Georgia*. Charleston, SC: Arcadia Publishing, 2000.

History of Macon: The First One Hundred Years, 1823–1923. Macon: *Telegraph*/InMedia, 2007. Orig. 1923.

Iobst, Richard W. *Civil War Macon*. Macon: Mercer University Press, 1999.

ISJL: Encyclopedia of Southern Jewish Communities. http://www.isjl.org/history/archive/

Macon's Black Heritage: The Untold Story. Macon: Tubman African American Museum, 1997.

Manis, Andrew. *Macon Black and White: An Unutterable Separation in the American Century*. Macon: Mercer University Press, 2004.

Prater, Vickie Leach. *Macon in Vintage Postcards*. Charleston, SC: Arcadia Publishing, 1999.

Simms, Kristina. *Macon, Georgia's Central City: An Illustrated History*. Chatsworth, CA: Windsor Publications for the Middle Georgia Historical Society, 1989.

Visit us at
arcadiapublishing.com

www.ingramcontent.com/pod-product-compliance
Lightning Source LLC
Chambersburg PA
CBHW050652110426
42813CB00007B/1988